THE MOON OF THE
WINTER
BIRD

THE THIRTEEN MOONS

The Moon of the Owls (JANUARY)

The Moon of the Bears (FEBRUARY)

The Moon of the Salamanders (MARCH)

The Moon of the Chickarees (APRIL)

The Moon of the Monarch Butterflies (MAY)

The Moon of the Fox Pups (JUNE)

The Moon of the Wild Pigs (JULY)

The Moon of the Mountain Lions (AUGUST)

The Moon of the Deer (SEPTEMBER)

The Moon of the Alligators (OCTOBER)

The Moon of the Gray Wolves (NOVEMBER)

The Moon of the Winter Bird (DECEMBER)

The Moon of the Moles (DECEMBER-JANUARY)

NEW EDITION   THE THIRTEEN MOONS

THE MOON OF THE WINTER BIRD

BY JEAN CRAIGHEAD GEORGE

ILLUSTRATED BY VINCENT NASTA

![HarperCollins logo] **HarperCollins**Publishers

The illustrations in this book
are oil paintings on masonite.

The Moon of the Winter Bird
Text copyright © 1969, 1992 by Jean Craighead George
Illustrations copyright © 1992 by Vincent Nasta

Typography by Al Cetta
1 2 3 4 5 6 7 8 9 10
NEW EDITION

Library of Congress Cataloging-in-Publication Data

George, Jean Craighead, date
    The moon of the winter bird / Jean Craighead George ;
illustrated by Vincent Nasta.—New ed.
        p.   cm. — (The Thirteen moons)
    Summary: During a cold spell in December, a song sparrow that
has not migrated south must adapt to the changes that winter
brings.
    ISBN 0-06-020267-X. — ISBN 0-06-020268-8 (lib. bdg.)
    1. Birds—Juvenile literature.   2. Birds—Wintering—Juvenile
literature.   3. Song sparrows—Wintering—Juvenile literature.
[1. Sparrows.   2. Birds.   3. Winter.]   I. Nasta, Vincent, ill.
II. Title.   III. Series: George, Jean Craighead, date, Thirteen
moons (HarperCollins)
QL795.B57G383   1992   91-15237
598.252′5—dc20   CIP
                                                         AC r91

Why is this series called The Thirteen Moons?

Each year there are either thirteen full moons or thirteen new moons. This series of books is named in their honor.

Our culture, which bases its calendar year on sun-time, has no names for the thirteen moons. I have named the thirteen lunar months after thirteen North American animals. Primarily night prowlers, these animals, at a particular time of the year in a particular place, do wondrous things. The places are known to you, but the animal moon names are not because I made them up. So that you can place them on our sun calendar, I have identified them with the names of our months. When I ran out of these, I gave the thirteenth moon, the Moon of the Moles, the expandable name December-January.

Fortunately, the animals do not need calendars, for names or no names, sun-time or moon-time, they follow their own inner clocks.

—JEAN CRAIGHEAD GEORGE

THE HALF MOON OF DECEMBER was obscured by a drizzling cloud layer that blanketed the Great Lakes states. The air was raw, cold, and growing colder. Beasts were in their dens, and birds were huddled on perches or in tree hollows. The longest night of the year was upon the land: December twenty-first.

This month was the moon of the winter bird. It is the month when the sun seems to stand still for several days at the winter solstice, December 21. On that day the Earth has carried the Northern Hemisphere as far away from the sun as it can go. As it starts back, all life seems to stand still like the sun, especially the winter bird.

On that evening of the solstice along the Olentangy River in Ohio, a blast of Arctic air turned the drizzle to ice. A row of glazed houses not far from the river glistened like holiday decorations in the glow of streetlights. One of the houses was yellow and almost square, the kind a child would draw. It creaked under the weight of the ice forming on its roof.

The house sat four hundred feet from the Olentangy River. Between it and the river lay an abandoned field where wild rye and sweet clover, goldenrod, teasel, and dandelions flourished in summer. Raspberry bushes and hawthorn trees speckled the field. Cottonwood trees bordered it along the river. A meadow wilderness, the field lured children to pick wild strawberries in the spring and to chase butterflies in the summer.

Around the yellow house a generous lawn met

the field in a carefree line of bushes: sumac, young maples, and alders. A toolshed and a bed of frost-blackened zinnias took up most of the side yard.

Close to the dining-room window grew a blue spruce tree. It was short, dense, and well pruned, and its limbs drooped as the drizzle on its needles turned to ice. A little sparrow, sleeping on a twig of the spruce, awoke. He cracked a frozen raindrop with his beak and moved two steps closer to the tree trunk. He went back to sleep.

He was a song sparrow, one of the most beautiful singers of America's fields and gardens. In spring and summer his voice explodes in bursts of trilling flute notes along roadsides, in yards, and in brushy fields. About two and a half inches high and gold-brown in color, he is not related to the house sparrows that hop on the city streets and nest in building cracks and eaves. The house sparrow came from Europe. The little songbird in the spruce was one of North America's thirty-four native sparrows. He and his kind spend their summers in thickets, meadows, field edges, and yards from southern Alaska across central Canada to Baja California, Mexico, and all across the United States from ocean to ocean. He is distinguished by his melodious song and the strong brown streaks on his sides and breast that converge into a sunburst on his chest.

The song sparrow should not have been in the spruce on this December night. Every other year he had been in Alabama with other song sparrows sleeping in bushes under warm, cloudless skies.

This year the Earth had not given him the message to leave. The declining daylight, which usually is one cue to migrate, did not set off his personal migration clock this year. He had watched the departure of the one half of the Olentangy song sparrow population that migrates each fall. The other half stays in the north. His young had taken off into the wind, striking out for lands they knew only through inherited knowledge; then his mate had flown south. The catbirds, bobolinks, tanagers, vireos, and blue-birds had left. All had flown with deliberateness, following their own compasses down the continent.

Yet the song sparrow of the yellow house had stayed. October was warm, his food abundant; and although the short hours of daylight had told him to go, he did not. The time to migrate came and went. By November it was too late. The light was wrong. The song sparrow could not go.

He became a "winter bird." He would stay in the cold with those of us who live in the north. In our backyards and fields he keeps us company while he waits for the Earth to stop traveling away from the sun and swing back to spring.

The sparrow, like all birds, woke up in the night. At ten o'clock he opened his eyes. He could barely see, for he was a daytime bird, but tonight

the gleaming ice around the streetlights caught his eye. Nervously he opened and closed his bill, as if trying to taste the meaning of the glitter.

His perch was the most sheltered spot on the tree. Out of the wind, it was warmed by the heat from the cellar window.

The drizzle stopped. The cold deepened. The spruce creaked and snapped under the heavy ice. The song sparrow dozed.

At six o'clock in the morning a buzz sounded above him. The alarm clock was ringing in the bedroom over his head. The light went on and the spruce tree sparkled. The song sparrow opened his eyes. Drowsily he listened, as he did every morning, to the ceremonial sounds of the people awakening. First came footfalls on the floor, then on the stairs. This was always followed by the clatter of pans in the kitchen. He had to wait a few minutes for the next noise, his cue to begin his day. Then it came. The door opened and the man of the house leaned down and picked up his morning paper. With that the song sparrow added to the droppings on the limb below him. The tidy pile told of the preciseness of his sleeping habits: that he slept every night in the same spot.

When the door closed, the song sparrow leaned down and peeked out into the yard through his "window" in the spruce twigs. He did this every morning in the winter, assessing the weather before deciding whether or not to get up. The Queen Anne's lace plants at the edge of the lawn were slick with ice. He puffed out his feathers and sat still.

The swatch of Queen Anne's lace was important to him. It was the focal point of his daily activities. Three Februarys ago he had made his first trip north. Beyond Columbus, Ohio, he had looked down on a brushy fence row and recognized the field where he had been raised. He did not stop, however—young birds rarely return

to their birthplaces. Nevertheless, the sight of his home slowed his flight. Ten miles farther north, he saw the broad swatch of last year's dry Queen Anne's lace. The seeds were a favorite food. He alighted on a dead flower head and looked around. He saw the yellow house, but primarily he saw the yard, the bushes, and the field. They were what he was seeking. They were song sparrow habitat. He scouted the area and then sat quietly.

As still as he was, a neighboring male song sparrow saw him. The neighbor flew at him, warning him to leave. The song sparrow was not intimidated. The patch of Queen Anne's lace and the yard were his. He faced his neighbor, who was perched on another dry flower head. Hunching low and puffing out his feathers menacingly, the neighbor assumed the "fight stance" of his species. Then they both flew at each other. They struck wings and beaks and, scolding, spiraled to

the ground. The challenger hopped onto his wings and flew back to his own territory. The battle was over. The song sparrow of the Queen Anne's lace had won.

He flew back to the dry flower heads and burst into song. His bubbling notes informed the challenger and all his neighbors that this patch was his.

Immediately, he flew to the spruce by the house and declared his ownership of the tree with another burst of song. He went on to claim the rosebush by the gate. Speeding to the top of the toolshed, he announced that it too belonged to him. He then darted into the field and sang on a hackberry bush; however, the bush belonged to the neighbor, who instantly sped at him with raised feathers. The neighbor reclaimed the hackberry bush and burst into volleys of song. The song sparrow flew to a raspberry bush not far from this enemy. Both birds sang until they settled on a "fence" between the two bushes beyond which they would not go. They then went off to roost.

For days the song sparrow sang from the Queen Anne's lace, the rosebush, the toolshed, and the raspberry bush. He flew around and around his property singing, announcing to the other song sparrow males that he owned this rich acre of land. The song fences were as real to him and his neighbors as our wire and wooden fences are to us. The birds respected them and stayed on their own property.

Setting up fences was not all the song sparrow was doing. He was also advertising for a mate. The migrating females were on their way north, for very few were winter birds. One morning in March they arrived.

The older female birds found their last year's mates. The younger ones quietly looked for the male with the best piece of property. That meant

land with many weeds for food, dense low bushes, and grass clumps for nesting sites. A good territory also had few predators such as foxes, snakes, cats, and the parasitic cowbirds.

Around noon, a female alighted in the rosebush. The song sparrow burst into song. She listened attentively. He flew around his property to show her how wealthy he was. He sang on the roof of the toolshed, on the dry stalk of Queen Anne's lace, and from the raspberry bush. The young female did not search farther. Instead, she preened her feathers. The song bird sang to her exuberantly from the Queen Anne's lace. When he was done, they broke seeds together. She pecked his beak. The song sparrow had found a mate.

Each year he had migrated south with his mate until this year, when he had turned into a winter bird. His life as a winter bird was good. Most of his neighbors were gone, and he was free to ignore fences and hunt over almost six acres of land. For the most part, he stayed on his own territory, where he knew the food sources and his enemies. This knowledge was his best defense against the cold. He only needed to fly over the toolshed to fill himself on beggar lice and dandelion seeds, or to drop into the cow parsnips for a meal. He knew where he could keep warm in folded clumps of leaves and where the house cat walked.

When the man of the house departed that icy morning and walked gingerly down the slippery path, the winter bird flitted to a higher branch in the tree and peeped out at the world. The street was glassy, the trees sparkled like crystal, and the air was cold. It chilled his bare feet. He pulled first one, then the other, into his warm breast feathers.

The morning was so bleak that the song sparrow stayed where he was. Automobile tires screamed as they spun on the ice. He flattened

his feathers to his body in fear. No sooner had he done so than the damp cold penetrated to his skin. Quickly he puffed, creating dead-air spaces, the best insulation known to human, bird, or beast. Soon he was warm.

The back door of the yellow house opened, and the cat came out. She stepped on the ice, slipped, turned, and rushed back inside before the door could close. The song sparrow knew the cat well. Black with white paws and penetrating yellow eyes, she was a formidable predator. Even the weasel and the black snake could not strike with the silent accuracy of the cat.

To protect himself, he had learned where she sunned and dozed. He had noted her pathways around his territory, and this knowledge had saved his mate.

Last April the song sparrow's mate had begun their nest in a clump of grass on the ground along the house cat's route. She had worked on it alone while the song sparrow stood guard. Usually he sang, but this time he clicked and scolded, warning her to leave. The warning only confused her. She worked harder, weaving grasses in and out of her nest and shaping it with her body for fifteen or twenty minutes each morning. She trilled as she worked. He clicked in distress. The morning the nest was finished, the cat walked down the trail. The song sparrow clicked, flicked his tail, and dove at the cat. The song sparrow's mate flew off and never returned to that site.

Because there were still no spring leaves to hide a nest in the bushes above the cat, the female began a new one under the dense, thorny raspberry bush where the cat did not walk. In three days she completed it. On the fourth day she lined it with fine grasses, and on the fifth day she laid an egg but did not incubate it. Each morning she would lay another egg until she had five; then she would settle down for ten days to incubate them.

After her first egg was laid, she joined the song sparrow in the fresh growing sprigs of Queen Anne's lace. They rested, then dropped to the footpath to bathe in the dust, for reasons known only to birds. While they were dusting, a female cowbird quietly stole through the raspberry bush and stepped down on the rim of their nest. The cowbird is a parasitic bird who lays her eggs in the nests of other birds and leaves them for the foster parents to raise. One of her favorite hosts is the song sparrow.

The cowbird jabbed the song sparrow's egg with her beak, flew off, and dropped it in the field. She returned to the empty nest and laid her own egg. Then she flew quickly off to hunt for other nests.

The female song sparrow returned to her nest the next morning to lay a second egg. She saw the cowbird egg, but because it was splotched and colored somewhat like her own, she ignored it.

She laid another egg and joined her mate.

A few minutes later the cowbird took the second egg away and laid her own. The next day the song sparrow's mate laid her third egg. When she departed, the cowbird arrived to take the third egg. She alighted on a low limb and looked down at the nest. She did not see the stalking cat. The cat swung her paw, and the song sparrows were rid of their enemy. Not only do cowbirds pierce the song sparrows' eggs, but their young grow faster. They either push the smaller song sparrow babies out of the nest or starve them to death by reaching higher to get all the food.

The song sparrow's mate also saw the cat. With a cry of alarm she deserted the nest full of cowbird eggs. She built her third nest deep in the now leafy raspberry bush, where no enemy could find it.

By the end of June the song sparrow and his mate had raised two broods of five babies each.

The song sparrow had helped to feed the young. Parent birds that look alike, such as song sparrows, blue jays, house wrens, and mourning doves, feed and tend their young. With parent birds such as cardinals, buntings, and robins, in which the males and females are markedly different, the females are in charge of building the nest, incubating, and rearing the young. Their males sing and guard the nest.

By the time the song sparrows' third brood was old enough to sun themselves and bathe—the last skills a young bird masters—it was August. The days were growing shorter, the internal clocks were ticking on toward October, and soon the winter bird would be alone.

On the day of the winter solstice, the winter bird, like the sun, seemed to be standing still. Long after he would have been up in the summer, he was still inactive. Two hours later he flew to the Queen Anne's lace, hovered over the icy surfaces, and flew on. He sped to the cow-parsnip patch. There under a dry leaf he found a dry twig to perch upon. Rumpled from the night, he began his morning preening. He took a feather in his bill and ran his beak down the shaft. The vanes opened and snapped back into place. Little barbs on the vanes locked with each other. He groomed his important flight feathers, then lifted each feather on his back and breast and aligned it with its neighbors. When he was done, he was not only streamlined for flight but insulated. The cold air could not penetrate his smooth cover. He looked down at his feet. A frozen droplet sparkled. He bit it, drank, and peered out from under the leaf.

The downy woodpecker, a resident bird that never migrates, was up. The bird called *pick, pick* from the elm tree, then, flying over the song sparrow, *yank*ed brightly. The sparrow flicked his tail but did not answer. The moon of

December had stilled his voice. He watched the woodpecker.

The driller alighted on the maple and hopped straight up it, defying gravity as he listened for insect larvae. Suddenly, he hammered with such force, it seemed his skull would break. But he does not even get a headache. A heavy coil of cartilage between his beak and skull absorbs the terrible impact—like shock absorbers in a car.

The song sparrow did not see the woodpecker drilling, nor did he see the woodpecker fish out a larva with a tongue twice the length of his head. The song sparrow was looking at a stalk of wild rye and feeling hungry. Flitting to it, he ran his beak along the head until he came to a seed. He turned it on end, cracked it, and ate it. He topped this off with some dandelion seeds. The ice on the knotweed seeds was too thick to crack. His meal ended.

Hopping back under the cow-parsnip leaf, he

fluffed his feathers and napped. Despite the cold the song sparrow was fatter in December than he had been all year. The snappy weather had increased his appetite, and with no nestlings to feed or song sparrow neighbors to fight, he had indulged himself in eating and taking fat-building naps. He was on hold, like the sun.

The woodpecker called again as he passed over the song sparrow. He was on his way to his hole in the apple tree by the gate. He did not like the icy weather and, having eaten, headed home. The woodpecker would climb down into his hole, where his body heat would soon raise the temperature inside the hole to a comfortable seventy degrees.

The song sparrow had no hole to keep him warm, and so he exercised. With quick wing strokes he flew to the toolshed, then to a fence post, where he rested. Below him a cottontail rabbit was licking the ice from between her toes.

A meadow vole was tunneling under the icy weeds. Out on the street a man and a boy held hands as they inched along the glassy pavement.

The song sparrow flew back to the toolshed roof just as a flock of winter song sparrows came to the field. He joined them. Many pairs of eyes were better at finding food in these harsh conditions than one pair. They all darted over the wild rye and ragweed. He veered and wheeled with them, then dropped down on the zinnia bed.

At noon he left the birds and flew to the spruce tree. The needles on the tree squeaked in the cold.

After a brief nap he joined the chickadees in the thistle patch in the field. The ice did not bother the chickadees. They are drillers, often making holes in trees. Hanging upside down, they pecked the ice from the thistles. The seeds took off in the wind on their little parachutes. The song sparrow followed them to the ground and ate them.

In the afternoon a wind arose, knocking the ice

on the trees and plants to the ground. A gray squirrel came down the elm tree, skidded over the ground, and dug up an acorn she had buried months ago. She stuffed it into her cheek and ran back to her leaf nest. The song sparrow flew to the Queen Anne's lace, now cleared of ice, and rested on a tough, old flower head before flying to the yard.

Late in the afternoon the temperature rose above freezing. The rain returned. The song sparrow flew to his spruce tree. Sidling along his limb, he felt with his feet for that special spot, found it, and settled down.

The gate to the yard creaked, and the woman of the house came home carrying an armload of brightly colored Christmas packages. As she opened the door of the yellow house, the cat ran out. He skidded on the wet steps, turned, and ran back.

The sparrow yawned. The fringe of fibrisse—

the bristlelike feathers growing at the base of his beak—trembled. These feathers are barometers of bird feelings. They stick out when the bird is agitated and fold back when it is calm. The song sparrow folded his fibrisse back.

Although it was still early, the temperature was dropping, and the winter bird was ready to retire. By bending his legs, he pulled a tendon that tightened his toes around the twig—now he would not fall in his sleep. The rain changed to snow.

Twilight descended. The wind howled. The streetlights came on. The man came home and stomped up the steps. As he opened the door, the song sparrow tucked his beak into the feathers on his back and went to sleep.

Around midnight the back door opened. The song sparrow awoke, as he did every night at this time. This was the cat's hour to hunt. She would prowl her pathways looking for mice and sleeping birds. The bird waited for her to come around the house, but she did not appear. She had skidded on the ice and was now yowling at the back door for the people to let her in.

The couple inside the house did not hear her over the wind, and eventually she stopped calling. Meowing in the cold, she sped along the side of the house to the cellar window beneath the spruce. The cat knew her property too. The windowsill was protected from the snow and wind by an overhang, and the windowpane was warmed by the heat in the house.

The song sparrow was alarmed. The cat was three feet below him, swinging her tail in anger.

The bird's fear protected him. Literally scared stiff, he could not move. Sitting still, he did not attract the attention of the cat, who relied on movement to see her prey. Although his feet grew cold, he did not pull them into his feathers. He did not scratch an itch. His life depended on

his sitting absolutely still.

An hour passed. The snow piled on the needles and limbs around the song sparrow. Still the bird did not move.

When a wind arose and drifted the snow, the cat tucked her front paws under her chest and squinted. Not comfortable enough to sleep, she dozed with eyes half open.

Fear was using up the song sparrow's reserve of fat. By two in the morning he had lost considerable weight. He was growing alarmingly cold. Still, he dared not move.

Suddenly he was warm. The snow had piled up around him, holding in his body heat like a warm blanket.

Three o'clock came and went, then four. The cat dozed. The bird sat still.

Inside the house, the alarm clock went off. Footsteps shook the floor, then the stairs. Pans rattled. The song sparrow did not wait for the door to open. He defecated. The cat looked up, saw him, and leaped. But he was gone, a snowy rocket headed for the raspberry patch.

The door opened. The cat dashed through the snow, up the steps, and into the house. The man leaned down, but there was no paper. The plows had not cleared his road. Smiling, he stretched and went back indoors.

Sinking into the powdery snow, the song sparrow panted in fear. His heart shook his entire body. Then he calmed down. Fear in birds is intense, but it does not last long. He flew to the dried ragweed stalks and ate his fill.

For the next several days while the sun seemed to stand still, the winter bird flitted and slept and ate.

On December 31, the moon of the winter bird was done. Another storm swirled in from the north. The woodpecker poked his head out of his hole and pulled it back in. The chickadees, roosting in the raspberry bush, did not get up. The squirrel rolled her head deeper into her belly fur and tail.

But into that wild cold morning flew the song sparrow. He was alert and bright. This day was eight minutes longer than on the day of the solstice. North America was spinning into the rays of the sun again, and the light was working its miracle. The winter bird was becoming a spring bird. A song was forming in his throat. He could not sing it out, but as December's moon went down behind the clouds, he cocked his head and listened toward the south.

Bibliography

Forbush, Edward Howe. *A Natural History of American Birds of Eastern and Central North America*. Boston: Houghton Mifflin Company, 1955.

National Geographic Society. *Field Guide to the Birds of North America*. Washington, D.C.: The National Geographic Society, 1987.

Nice, Margaret Morse. *Studies in the Life History of the Song Sparrow*, Vols. I and II. New York: Dover Publications, Inc., 1937, 1943.

Pettingill, Olin Sewall, Jr. *Ornithology in Laboratory and Field*. Minneapolis, Minn.: Burgess Publishing Company, 1970.

Index